HOW TO MAKE A PERFECT CUP OF COFFEE

Everything you need to
know to brew a killer
coffee every single time

VINH NGUYEN

CONTENTS

INTRODUCTION

I am a coffee lover.

OK, I admit it! I am coffee obsessed. Coffee is the first thing I think of in the morning, and it is the energy I need to get on with my day.

For me, there is nothing quite like waking up in the morning, rushing to the kitchen, and brewing that first perfect cup of coffee. The aroma and the taste just make me go all super-excited about the day ahead.

Perhaps you feel the same about coffee? Otherwise, you wouldn't be reading this book.

Of all the drinks in the world, coffee seems to have universal appeal. But if you have ever traveled, you'd quickly discover that one person's coffee could be quite different from another's. My perfect cup of coffee may be your worst ever.

So join me on this journey to learn more about this god-sent gift called coffee:

- How was it discovered?
- Are there health benefits?
- What are innovative ways to brew a perfect cup of coffee?
- How to choose and maintain a coffee maker?

My hope is that upon completion of this book, you will be inspired to find a new and fun way to create your perfect cup of coffee.

But before you continue, I have a confession to make. I am Vietnamese and have a soft spot for Vietnamese coffee and strong espresso. So you will notice that in this book, I may talk more about these coffees.

Now that's out of the way, let's move on discovering more about this drink together (perhaps with a cup of coffee?)!

CHAPTER 1

COFFEE FACTS

"Coffee, the favorite drink of the civilized world."
— Thomas Jefferson

A brief history in time

It is probably common knowledge that coffee was discovered in Ethiopia. The "red" cherries, which the sheep ate and became very active, were taken home and tasted. What was known as the devil's fruit became coffee as the world knows it today. Another tale that has been around for some time involves an Arabian who used coffee beans to survive an exile and was discovered near the town of Mocha. So, we now refer to one of the coffees as "mocha."

There is a lot of history and legends about coffee, creating a mystique for the beverage. Famous luminaries seem to have had some kind of brush with the drink. And it is said that the Boston Tea Party, so well-known for throwing away boxes of tea, considered coffee drinking a patriotic act.

Coffee remained in Arabia for quite some time and was a secret that Arabians were not keen to share with outsiders. India was one of the first few countries outside Arabia to get a taste of coffee. From then on, there was no holding back for the popularity of this drink.

Coffee is now grown in around eighty countries in South and Central America, the Caribbean, Africa, and Asia. All of the regions that grow coffee are in tropical zones within 30 degrees or so of the equator.

Many famous words and trends have been the output of coffee as it gets accepted as part of the global culture. Countries like Brazil have an entire economy dependent on coffee production, and the United States is one of the largest coffee drinking nations in the world.

And did you know that Vietnam is the second-biggest coffee producer in the world?

Robusta versus Arabica

Coffee, or Coffea in scientific terms, is part of a family of flowering plants called Rubiaceae. The seeds of these Coffea species are what we know as coffee beans.

There are over 120 species of Coffea, but the beans we use to make the drink fall into two main types: Arabica and Robusta. Arabica has a smoother and sweeter taste, while Robusta contains nearly double the caffeine content and has a more bitter taste. Robusta is usually used in espresso blends because it creates a better foam layer on the top of an espresso shot.

Many coffee makers blend Robusta with Arabica to create their own unique flavors. The quality of the coffee is dependent on the proportions of the mix of these beans.

Robusta coffee is reported to make up about 97 percent of Vietnam's total coffee production.

An introduction to Vietnamese coffee

It is said that in 1857, a French Catholic priest first brought coffee to Vietnam. However, Vietnam didn't become a major coffee exporter until the country opened its economy to the world through a political and economic renewal campaign ("Đổi Mới") in 1986. Now, there are many coffee plantations in the central highlands of Vietnam, thanks to the region's climate and soil conditions ideal for growing coffee. Vietnam now dominates the coffee industry in Southeast Asia and is the Number 1 producer of Robusta coffee in the world.

People typically think of "Vietnamese coffee" as the iced coffee with sweetened condensed milk ("cà phê sữa đá"), made with a Vietnamese coffee drip filter ("phin cà phê"). This popular beverage came about when there was not much fresh milk available in Vietnam, so the French and Vietnamese began to stir their dark roast coffee with sweetened condensed milk and pour over crushed ice to enjoy during hot weather.

Vietnamese coffee is generally very strong because the majority of the coffee made in Vietnam is from Robusta beans. Although "cà phê sữa đá" is widely seen as "traditional Vietnamese coffee," the locals enjoy many other ways of making coffee accordingly to various regions and climates throughout the year. You can even find Vietnamese egg coffee ("cà phê trứng") in many cafes in Hanoi, the capital of Vietnam. It is made with Robusta coffee, egg yolk, and sweetened condensed milk. People typically compare the taste and texture of Vietnamese egg coffee to those of tiramisu or eggnog.

CHAPTER 2

COFFEE & HEALTH

"Three cups of coffee a day keeps the doctor away."
— Anonymous

Does caffeine reduce the risk of liver disease and boost memory?

Caffeine, like chocolate, often receives bad publicity. While in some instances, and in excess, these can have negative effects on our body, they can also be quite beneficial.

Of course, some people are more sensitive to the negative effects of caffeine. For example, excess caffeine can create anxiety, nausea (particularly if taken on an empty stomach), an increased heart rate, and even depression in some people.

But scientists have turned up some interesting facts on caffeine. For example, caffeine blocks the effects of a neurotransmitter in the brain ("adenosine") that otherwise makes us feel tired. This is why it works so well to keep us awake. It also encourages the release of another brain chemical called "dopamine" that contributes to a feeling of well-being.

Two studies found that drinking caffeine-containing drinks like coffee and tea had a protective effect for those at risk of developing liver disease. The results showed that people who drank more than two cups of coffee a day had a 44% lower chance of showing actual liver damage than those who drank no caffeine. This was not a clinical trial, and the reason why coffee and tea had such an effect is unknown. Coffee and tea contain a range of plant chemicals ("phytonutrients") that could be responsible for this.

A 2005 Norwegian study also found similar benefits for coffee with regards to liver disease. Accordingly to this study, drinking three cups of coffee a day could lower the risk of death from liver cirrhosis.

Even if you're not at risk of liver disease, caffeine still has some advantages. Recent research from Austria showed that caffeine may enhance short-term memory. Researchers found an increase in brain activity in the parts of the brain associated with memory and attention. These parts of the brain were the frontal lobe and the anterior cingulum. An earlier study (2004) found that caffeine did support short-term memory, but only when it was related to a topic that people were already thinking about. This study found that when testing coffee's effects on unrelated subjects, short-term recall was actually inhibited.

Everything does have a flip side, though. Adenosine, which is blocked by coffee, is also calming. This could be why it can also cause anxiety in some individuals. After all, the balance of our brain chemistry is unique, and when we are addicted to stimulants like caffeine, we lose sensitivity to our natural stimulants such as dopamine and adrenaline.

Can coffee reduce the risk of diabetes?

Diabetes is a disorder characterized by hyperglycemia or elevated blood glucose (blood sugar). Our bodies function best at a certain level of sugar in the bloodstream. If the amount of sugar in our blood runs too high or too low, we typically feel bad.

With diabetes, the body does not produce or properly use insulin—a hormone needed to convert sugar, starches, and other food into energy needed for daily life. The cause of diabetes is a mystery, although genetics and environmental factors such as obesity and lack of exercise appear to play roles.

Research suggests that people who drink coffee are less likely to get type 2 diabetes. It isn't known whether caffeine or some other ingredient in coffee is responsible for its protective effects.

The researchers wanted to see whether there is a link between diabetes and drinking beverages such as coffee and green, black, and oolong tea. Participants completed a detailed questionnaire about their health, lifestyle habits, and how much coffee and tea they drank. The questionnaire was repeated at the end of the five-year follow-up period.

When other factors were accounted for, researchers found that the more green tea and coffee participants drank, the less likely they were to get diabetes. People who drank three cups of coffee or more (or six cups of green tea or more) each day were about one-third less likely to get diabetes. The link was more notable in women than in men. No pattern was seen with black or oolong tea.

What about other health concerns?

While coffee may be one of the most popular drinks around, millions are forced to do without it because of heartburn, acid reflux, or stomach discomfort. This is because coffee does increase acid in the stomach, which causes some gastrointestinal issues.

However, not all is bad news for those with sensitive stomachs. These people can opt for lower acidity or dark roast coffee, which is reported to be easier on the stomach. Adding milk may also help to lower your stomach sensitivity. In this way, they can still enjoy coffee, especially when they need it to focus better while benefiting from coffee's antioxidant qualities.

In addition to caffeine being known to help asthmatics prevent attacks, recent studies have shown coffee consumption can have several other health benefits. Drinking coffee has been associated with a lower risk of gallstone disease in men, reduced risk of kidney stone formation, and a reduced risk of colon cancer.

Other studies have found coffee to be a good source of potassium, promoting the effectiveness of migraine medications and a way of protecting against free-radical damage to tissues. One study found it had more antioxidant activity than red wine, green or black tea, or orange juice.

CHAPTER 3

COFFEE BREWING

"Coffee smells like freshly ground heaven."
— Jesse Lane Adams

Six ways to brew coffee

Now that you have learned a bit about the history of coffee and its health benefits, let's take a look at six primary ways of brewing coffee. Each method has brewing variables—introducing water, brewing temperature, and separating the brewed liquor from the coffee grounds.

"Turkish" brewing: Turkish coffee ("kahve") is made in small containers, with water and finely ground kahve boiled on the flame. It is often brewed up with sugar already introduced. In some traditions, they pour a little bit of brewed coffee into each cup first, bring it to a second boil, then pour the rest into each cup again. This is to ensure an even distribution of grounds. In some regions, they serve the kahve with added spice, which is usually cardamom. The coffee is not filtered from the liquor, leaving a thick, pungent, and muddy brew. The mud settles to the bottom of the tiny demitasse cups the coffee is served in. In many countries, they read the coffee mud after you have drunk your coffee and tell you your future.

Concentrate brewing: Concentrate brewing is very popular in Latin America and other parts of the world. It is beginning to make a comeback in the United States. This method takes large amounts of coffee brewed with small amounts of water to brew a concentrate. To make a cup of coffee, you mix some of the concentrate with hot water. The concentrate is brewed, either hot or cold. When it is brewed cold, you must let the coffee sit for at least a day. This method creates a mild light-bodied coffee with little aroma and acidity and a muted flavor.

Percolating: This procedure involves a continuous brewing of the coffee grounds using boiling water, which turns to boiling coffee liquor brewing over the grounds. Some argue that this makes a good cup of coffee, while others say this style of brewing makes the worst coffee imaginable. The naysayers exclaim this method produces a bitter coffee, no matter what brand or grind of coffee you use.

Auto-drip: This is the most popular way to brew coffee in the United States. It's simple—pouring hot water over grounds in a filter and letting the brew drip through a filter. Drip brewing can produce an excellent cup of coffee if the proper equipment is used. One of the biggest issues with auto-drip machines is they don't brew at the right temperature. If you have a good auto-drip brewing machine, then the next hurdle to tackle is the filter. Paper filters can deposit a flavor in the coffee and do not allow many of the coffee oils and organic compounds through. A gold-plated reusable filter is a perfect option for drip brewing. It will not deposit a taste in the coffee and doesn't trap as much of the coffee's essence as paper filters do.

French press: French press brewing gives you complete control. Although it is more labor-intensive than auto-drip, the brewing variables can be better controlled. You place coarsely ground coffee in a glass carafe and pour hot water over the grounds. When the brewing is complete, you use a plunger that consists of a metal mesh plate to push the grounds to the bottom. The coffee liquor is on top, ready to be poured off. The mesh filter allows the oils and fine coffee particles through without a problem.

Vietnamese coffee drip: This brewing method can be seen as a combination of French press and drip brewing procedures, using a Vietnamese coffee filter ("phin"). To brew, you add ground coffee into the chamber of the filter and press it down with an insert. Then, you pour hot water over the grounds and let it drip slowly over several minutes. Robusta beans work best with this brewing procedure because Arabica beans seem to turn slightly sour in this filter. The taste and how long it takes to brew may also vary, depending on the type of grounds and the pressure you put onto the grounds.

How to grind coffee

One of the critical elements to make a perfect cup of coffee is the right grind to the right brewing method. So, let's see how we can grind your coffee beans properly.

Air is the enemy of all coffee drinkers. Once air comes in contact with your coffee, they begin to lose their flavor. Coffee manufacturers vacuum-seal their coffees to keep them fresh while they sit on the shelves at the supermarket. However, once you break that seal, it's all downhill from there.

Buying whole coffee beans and grinding them yourself is a great way to ensure that your coffee

remains as flavorful as possible.

Different types of coffee call for different types of grind. So you'll need to learn to use your coffee grinder properly if you want to make the freshest coffee possible.

If you plan on brewing your coffee with a percolator or a French press coffee maker, then you'll need a coarser grind. Place the coffee beans in your coffee grinder and tap the grind button a few times as you would use the pulse feature on your food processor. The goal is to break the beans up so that they look like tiny pieces of coffee beans. If they look like powder, you need to slowly back away from the coffee grinder and start again. Remember to tap the button and not hold it down.

Auto-drip coffee makers work best with medium grinds. Picture the grinds that you'd find in a can of supermarket coffee. Those are medium grinds. They can be described as looking like brown sand. Remember the last time you went to the beach, but instead of seeing the sand in between your toes, imagine seeing sand in your coffee maker. Once again, while holding the coffee grinder button, don't get carried away and over-grind your coffee beans. You do not want a fine powder if you're going to use an automatic coffee maker.

When using an espresso maker, you want those fine powdery grinds that you've been trying to avoid when making coarse and medium grinds. So grind away until your heart is content.

Finally, if you are using a Vietnamese coffee filter, it's best to use a medium-coarse grind. This grind will make sure that you don't have to wait forever for the water to drip all down, and there is no residue in your cup.

Grinding your coffee beans right before you brew your coffee is a great way to make sure that you're getting the freshest cup of coffee possible.

How to brew coffee

Brewing a perfect cup of coffee depends on several things, such as the quality of the coffee beans, the quality of the water being used, the type of brewing being done, and the grind of the coffee. The quality of beans and water is something you can easily take care of—just use good quality beans and pure water. However, the relationship between the grind of the coffee and the type of brewing is more detailed and could use a little explanation.

Now we all know that we make coffee by passing hot water over crushed coffee beans. However, we need to understand just how long the water should be passing over the beans to yield a perfect cup of coffee. You need to know how to match your coffee's grinds to the types of brewing you are doing to make the best coffee possible.

Generally speaking, the "soaking" time relates directly to how coarse the coffee is ground. This means that smaller coffee grinds need less contact with the water, and coarser grinds need longer contact. Espresso coffee uses very fine ground coffee, so it should only be exposed to water for 20-40 seconds. A French press coffee maker can take as much as four minutes and uses an extremely coarse grind. If coffee is left in contact with water for longer than needed for its grind size, unwanted extracts emerge and make the coffee taste bitter. Of course, if the grind is too large and the water passes very quickly (like using a French press grind in an espresso maker), very little of the caffeine and flavors is extracted.

In a Vietnamese coffee filter, water is poured in two stages: the first pour fills up about a quarter of the filter for the coffee to absorb and expand for about 30 seconds, then the second pour follows. The first pour "wakes up" the aroma and flavors of the coffee, while the second pour "completes" it.

Brewing a cup of coffee is not that hard. Brewing a perfect cup of coffee takes a little more understanding but isn't any harder. Start with fresh beans and good clean water, match your brewing style to the proper grind, and then mess around with the exact proportions. Pretty soon, you will be brewing a killer coffee every single time.

CHAPTER 4

COFFEE MAKERS

"My coffee machine is the most beautiful person in the world to me."
—Anonymous

Coffee maker types

When we hear the term "coffee maker," most of us think of only one type of coffee maker. Most often, the drip-style coffee maker or the espresso-type machine comes to mind, depending on where you live and your taste in coffee. One type of coffee maker may be frowned upon in certain parts of the world while being quite acceptable in another location.

Some types of coffee makers are quite antiquated by

today's standards but are still being used by those who prefer the coffee made their way. Such is the case with the percolator-style coffee makers. There are two types of percolator-style coffee makers: the stovetop model and the electric percolator. Both percolators work in the same fashion, which is circulating boiling water over the coffee grounds and through a metal filter repeatedly.

The auto-drip coffee maker is by far the most recognized type of coffee maker. These coffee makers usually have a heating element to keep the brewed coffee reasonably hot until the coffee is gone or it's time to brew another pot. Some models come with a thermal style carafe, which allows the coffee drinker to brew a pot of coffee right into the carafe for coffee on the go. The auto-drip coffee maker also has the versatility to make from one to ten cups of coffee at a time. It uses disposable filters, unlike the percolator-style coffee makers.

The espresso coffee maker comes in two versions for the consumer, stovetop and electric. The stovetop model is less expensive than its electric counterpart. The stovetop espresso maker is also highly portable, while the electric model is limited in mobility by its size and requires electricity.

One drawback to the stovetop espresso coffee maker is that it may leave bits of very fine powdery granules. This makes the stovetop espresso coffee maker a device, the techniques of which one must master to get a perfect cup of coffee.

A Vietnamese coffee filter is traditionally made of aluminum, but nowadays, you can find many stainless steel filters in many sizes. They are all portable, easy to clean, and do not take much space in your kitchen. A phin is meant to be single-served, so it's best to buy multiple small-size filters if you are to share your Vietnamese coffee experience with friends and family.

From coffee makers to espresso

As I confessed at the beginning of the book, I have a soft spot for a strong espresso shot (apart from Vietnamese coffee). So in this section, let me talk a little more about it and help you find a perfect coffee maker for espresso.

Espresso is made by high heat and pressure, which produces a thicker and more potent cup of coffee. It is usually served in much smaller cups and quantities because of how strong it is.

Electric machines are making their way from the restaurant into many home kitchens. The cleaning and care, including the job to decalcify, are made easier by the popularity of stainless steel appliances. There are also coffee makers that do all of the jobs of creating the perfect mug of coffee right on your countertop and even while you sleep. The grind and brew combination machines are the ideal way to get the freshest cup of coffee possible.

To get a perfect espresso, consider making your own at home instead of running to your local coffee shop or favorite corner cafe. If the thought of becoming a kitchen barista has you shaking without any caffeine, think again! There are a wide variety of espresso machines geared for home use, from the basic to the same machines used by the professionals.

However, before you drop a couple of hundred dollars on that top-of-the-line espresso machine, consider your options and needs. If you are experiencing sticker shock from some of the higher-end espresso machines, keep in mind that you are saving a great deal daily by avoiding high-priced indulgences at coffee shops or cafes.

The first thing you should know before choosing a home espresso machine is that there are various types of machines. Each type will come with a different price tag and different capabilities. Although the top-of-the-line machine may be nice, it may not necessarily meet your needs. Instead of buying an espresso machine simply because it is deemed "the best," buy a machine that you can (and will) use regularly.

Here are different types of home espresso machines:

Pump espresso: Typically found in a coffee shop, a pump espresso machine is usually made for commercial purposes but can be used in your home. Be prepared to expand your budget since they are typically the priciest of the bunch. Also, pump espresso machines are usually the largest, heaviest, and noisiest of the options, but it produces a fantastic cup of espresso. These machines work by using a pump to keep the water pressure at an appropriate level.

Piston espresso: If you are looking for a great, low-maintenance espresso machine, consider those that run on a piston or lever system. Instead of a pump to create pressure, these machines use a level to maneuver and create steam. Although a piston espresso machine is very quiet, it may require a great deal of arm strength to pull on the lever continually. Furthermore, the piston espresso machine can make a great cup of espresso, but it may take practice to get the hang of the process.

Steam espresso: Using steam to create pressure to make the espresso, these steam-powered espresso machines are typically the type found in the home. With smaller machines that occupy less space and cost less money, steam espresso machines are relatively quick and easy to use. However, keep in mind that the steam produced may not provide the appropriate pressure, so the steam level should be constantly maintained.

Moka pots: Moka pots are a stovetop method to produce espresso. The process is simple and easy, although the final product may be less than professional. Using a specially-designed, two-part pot, the steam produced by the water boiling in the bottom of the pot is forced into the top part of the pot, where the coffee is boiling. It requires less pressure than the other types of home espresso machines, but there is no milk frothing or foaming attachments, so you may have to sacrifice that feature for price and size.

Any one of these different types of home espresso machines will allow you to make a delicious cup of espresso. Your choice should be based on needs, usability, the overall size of the machine, and of course, the price.

Cleaning your coffee maker

The last tip to make sure you brew a killer coffee anytime is to clean your coffee maker.

Did you know that your coffee maker could be killing you? Well, it is, if your morning cup of coffee is a matter of life and death, and you have a filthy coffee maker.

When was the last time you thoroughly cleaned your coffee maker? Washing the pot is essential but getting the internal components of a coffee maker clean is a task that you shouldn't skip. **A clean coffee maker can be the difference between a good cup of coffee and a nasty cup of sludge.**

A clean coffee maker can affect how your coffee tastes. Leftover coffee oils can accumulate inside your coffee maker. Also, mineral deposits can form, especially in areas with hard water. These deposits are called "scale." There are two kinds of scale, limescale and mineral scale—and you don't want either of them. Scale can affect the heating unit and the water flow of your coffee maker and reduce its efficiency. How quickly scale forms depends on the quality of your drinking water. If you use bottled water to make your coffee, the scale probably won't form as fast, but you still have to worry about accumulated coffee oils. Better to play it safe and clean your coffee maker regularly.

Cleaning your coffee maker is not a hard task to accomplish. It's as easy as making coffee. All you have to do is pour a pot of half vinegar and half water into the coffee maker's water reservoir (white vinegar should be used). Steer clear of the red wine or apple cider vinegar varieties. Then just turn on the regular brew cycle. Your kitchen will probably have a pleasant salad smell, which you may even like. If you're not a salad fan, though, remember that it's a small price to pay for a good cup of coffee.

Now rinse the coffee maker out by using only water this time and running the brew cycle again. You may have to do this a few more times if you still smell the vinegar.

Another easy way to keep the coffee maker clean is to put a glass marble in the water chamber. All the mineral deposits that would usually accumulate inside the coffee maker will instead accumulate on the marble. Occasionally, just remove the marble, wash it and then place it back in the chamber. How much easier could that be?

The best solution would be to clean your coffee maker with vinegar monthly while also using the marble method. Change the marble once a week, and your coffee maker will be in great shape.

If you have an old coffee maker and you aren't happy with the taste of its brew, why not try cleaning it.

A clean coffee maker will brew a perfect cup of coffee (well, together with the techniques you've just learned from this book).

AUTHOR NOTE

Thank you for reading this book! I hope you have been energized and are ready to make another perfect cup of coffee, perhaps in a new and innovative way?

One thing before you go. I have a wee story to tell you.

For years, as a fan of Vietnamese coffee and espresso, I was frustrated not being able to find a coffee product that really gave me high energy, yet contained no artificial ingredients. So I created a coffee brand to deliver just that: "100% pure - 100% Vietnamese" Robarica Coffee.

However, don't take my word for it! If you want to try it, you can get it on amazon.com—the coffee is currently only available in the United States: www.robarica.com

As a special thanks to you, here's an offer (hopefully, you can't resist): just apply the Coupon Code G2PT7OUS on your checkout, and you can get a 50% discount. (Note that this Coupon Code is only available for a limited time.)

Thanks again, and enjoy!

Vinh Nguyen

P/S: Don't forget to make yourself a perfect cup of coffee and write a review on Amazon for this book and/or Robarica Coffee: www.amazon.com/ryp

ABOUT THE AUTHOR

Vinh Nguyen is a self-confessed coffee addict. His goal is to make you become one, as well.

Vinh was born and bred in Vietnam, and lives (happily ever) in New Zealand.

Printed in Great Britain
by Amazon